T0124435

'HELL-P ME'

'HELL-P ME'

POEMS

2016-2017

LITTLE GRAPE JELLY

GRACE PILKINTON

LILY ASHLEY

JAMES MASSIAH

First published in 2017
by Eyewear Publishing Ltd
Suite 333, 19-21 Crawford Street
Marylebone, London WIH IPJ
United Kingdom

Cover illustration by Chingis Guirey
Cover design and typeset by Edwin Smet

Author photograph by Lily Bertrand-Webb

Printed in England by TJ International Ltd, Padstow, Cornwall

All rights reserved
© 2017 Lily Ashley, Grace Pilkington & James Massiah

The right of the authors to be identified as author of
this work has been asserted in accordance with section 77
of the Copyright, Designs and Patents Act 1988

ISBN 978-1-911335-92-4

*Eyewear wishes to thank Jonathan Wonham for his
generous patronage of our press.*

WWW.EYEWEARPUBLISHING.COM

Lily Ashley is a poet and playwright whose one-woman, sell-out show at the Vaults Festival, 'You Are Me And I Am You', made women cry and men apologise.

Grace Pilkington is a feminist poet who has performed on the BBC World Service. Her essay 'Sugar-Coated' was long-listed for the Notting Hill Editions Essay Prize.

James Massiah is a poet who has performed at The Southbank Centre, Tate Modern, Queen Elizabeth Olympic Park and the Houses of Parliament.

From: Lily Ashley
Subject: Hell-p me
Date: Tue, 12 Jul 2016 13:22:00
To: Dear Grace and James, it is with the most
immense amount of enthusiasm that I kick off our
project.

the water is winning today
whipping whiners into wails of whys
i can hear their cries
from my dark and darker room
i lose hope too soon
shriek shriek repeat
wrong shoes, soggy feet
wrong mood, wrong way
contact today
trying to avoid the reality
trying to avoid he reality
they haven't called
they haven't thought
they haven't cared dared or shared
why and where and how and who
they're moving on without a clue
and all that's left is me to do
and do and do and do and do
avoid
the boy
avoid the boy
boy boy boy
oi oi oi oi oi oi oi oi oi oi oi oi oi oi oi oi oi oi oi oi oi

Oink, oink, oink Leaves our PM
Heavy clouds spell MAY But it's July.
I put a small pink straight jacket on my heart this morning,
Because it leaps and shakes and jumps and aches
You can trust me with your child I said, I am here to educate.
I wore my maternal guise,
While she was baptized,
Now I return to behind my screen
And watch my curser flicker,
Waiting for a letter
Like tomorrow's tutee.

why's a straight jacket on your heart?
ugh
i can't think just need women to mend me
men to mend me
i need James
i need you and i need James to mend me, this, make it make sense today
take me away today
ugh
what letter are you waiting for?
ugh
i got to go, closing up
shutting up
because nothing makes sense today
everything's dull today
stained and dull today
rained on world today
pained dumb girl today
I'm getting lots of messages saying it's hard today
think i'll just delete this dreary day...
what letter are you waiting for?

From: James Massiah

Date: Thu, 14 Jul 2016 08:02:03

Two letters
Actually
A and E
They govern me
And light the way
My jackets straight
My brothers bi
And I am gay
In the happiest way
Say hi to girls
And back they wave
Hit it from the back, they say
And I'll be back
To terminate
Contracts I had
With prior mates
From yesterday
And yesterday
And yesterday
And yesterday
I'm black and proud
And not ashamed
The blackest cloud
Will bring the rain
I am the master of my race
My gender, sex, my class, my face
My friends
My foes
My fucks
My lays

A different time
When things were not like
Now they be
That's when you asked me
Why I be
The way I be
I said it be's
Because of all the
Things I've seen

Are multicoloured
Plenty shades
And in the rain
We'll dance all day
And dance all night
Till kingdom came
And when it came
I felt to cry
It took me back

I want to know the way you be,
The things you've seen.
I walked past A and E
To the late night GP
The world crashed and tears
Fled from my eyes,
So now I am to be mended
By a woman who prescribed
Small pink and white pills
Because my mind was ill
And each evening as it slips down my throat
I can't help but think it's one big joke,
Taking something everyday,
Just to be
Me.
But I was stifled by darkness
And they were pink and luminous and bright.
You see – I treat all that happened prior,
With propriety and priority.
I think about ex-jobs, ex-lives, ex
So living today,
Today living is hard.
The today when our country falls into the hands of May
And a racist, sexist fumbling fool appears to join her in her rule?
The Independent flashes new news every minute,
And I twitch, I'm suddenly an addict to cabinet reshuffling,
Guess it's just today's way of giving the inner voice a muffling.

I can't pick up the paper
Won't pick up that drummed dumb
               book of scum
Scare us please
      I plea
 Control us
Don't let us see
Don't let us think of bright
        Only fear at night
      Of riot racist terror treats
Pinning us to our urined seats
Keeping eyes to ourselves
Keeping friendships held and held
And never seeing past the thought
     Of panic driving fight to fought
       Of eyes of sorrow seen as cold
So we're destined death alone and old
And they prescribe those pills of bubble gum
       And promise that they'll bring you fun
    But grace you fill me with such ideas
That you need anything brings me years and tears   and wonder what the fuck?
                      and why are we so bloody stuck
On fitting in on   holding back on fucking cunts
        so fucking wack
          and SACKED it says cross the front page
            no longer will they have a wage
               but fuck a wage
I mean what yes I don't
but ah come on   a wage
a sense of fucking worth?
that you can only find in a purse?!

Then a person at a house party
Gave me a line and asked if I
Could help them find a pill
The kind that cures all ills
Until it's thrills cease to seal
The serotonin to the cell
Was feeling whack
Now shit is dope
The dopamine floats
I feel like I can cope
I've turned a stoic
It's as though I'll never
Be too high or low
And so we go
To tread the water
Seeking balance
And a bow
For the arrows in my quiver
Are much sharper now
Ergo

yea, i remember that
last weekend
last year everything was so clear
stand alone it told me
stand alone and feel the breeze
like a ram, looking cross the valley for sheep
no panic, just pride, stood alone, no bleat
but i sunk down into him
sunk down and tried to pick a corpse of secrets out of an infested hole
an invested hole
where they'd decided they'd steal another soul
rolling round in words that belonged to others
my lover
my lover
i became their mother
i wanted to save
desperate to cure
you do   don't you
when you start loving them more
loving it more
that addictive chore
of picking up   picking up
tell them they're better
all of your work becomes a love letter
all of yourself gets alienated
and when you look in the mirror it reflects who is hated
i can't get away from the cunt love addiction
can't move on from this stereotyped fiction
ah
ah
ah
ah

I know the sinking,
stinking thinking
late night drinking,
and surrendering
entirely to some notion
of 'we',
tearing 'I' out
like a tree,
ripped from the ground.
Planting seeds of expectation,
in ego earth
which can never fertilise,
or nourish,
only wilt and fall.
This morning, I saw a fox
intestines torn out,
blood dripping across the junction,
A Jack the Ripper of foxes on the prowl,
but whereas 2 weeks ago,
my head would've dropped its
tear-stained cheeks,
today I looked up,
and saw the sun peeking
through the clouds

From: Lily Ashley
Sent: 16 July 2016 22:08
Subject: Re: Hell-p me

CALL ME YOU JERK
CALL ME CALL ME CALL ME
CALL ME YOU ARE ABOUT TO LEAVE
PLEASE CALL ME YOU JERK AND
JERK OFF JERK OFF
JERK OFF!!!!!

Jerking off to something foxy
Fantasies start to feature blood in the mix
Watching videos from nature reserves
Only serves to increase the desire to witness violence
from a distance love from a distance sex from a distance
life from a distance
earth from a distance
you from a distance
this from a distance
and i distinctly remember
being asked to speak more succinctly
by my fathers in the funk
to be more direct and clear
when demanding positions in sex
and working out the payment terms
on invoices and the clearing of cheques
this year i will be more assertive
i will eat less dessert
i will do what i want
to who i want
when i want
because they probably deserve it
in accordance with some arbitrary law
of fiction
never forget the story
about giving shines in the kitchen
coming on the stove
mother being horrified
but wiping it up

and continuing as if it
never occurred
years go by and
so do a million unsaid words
but this year i will speak my mind
and of that i am certain
this will be the year
the holy ghost tears the curtain

On 18 Jul 2016, at 17:18, Grace Pilkington
wrote:

I feel as if I'm living life from a distance,
pollen itches my eyes and twitches my nose,
I want to cut them off.
My mind is broken and tired,
I slept for fifteen hours,
tucked away neatly
in the land of death.
Still my body aches for sleep.
celebrating marriage again
I sat with an ex and tried to be civilised
as we discussed our new separate lives
He tore my heart out, swung it around
and hung it on his keyring.
But with time, I took it off
and slipped it back in,
next to my lungs,
I've never mastered assertiveness
always too tired.
Too tired.
Too tired,
wired
and then too tired.

I think we might have something interesting here
something worth investigating
cos our connection has been slow/faulty
with this keyboard and this screen between us
this futureless context controlled by wifi speed
controlled by personal means
no eyes to watch and read
no tone to hear and gauge
just tap tap and re-read
tap tap and re-read
communication good and bad
communication   virtual   sad
but i wrote it happy
or but i wrote it heavy
but you read it blue and read it yellow
read furious rage as calm and mellow
did you?   did you?   forget to respond?
but a door opening and someone leaving
a door opening and someone leaving
is noticeable   is noticed
and questioned and out of hand
connecting like this
connecting like this... can it work?
does it work?
can you understand me? really really really understand me, can you?
with this written automania... this splurging like speech but onto
      a page of pixels
where my cries, screams and smiles won't be found till overground
      at a cafe,

or at home with enough time to read
to listen and to respond
my emotions no longer jeopardise your day
you can walk out   you can walk away
knowing you will still be a support
your responses never come up short
but by the time you've got back, by the time you've replied
I've rubbed the glue off my skin and the sea from my eyes.
So soft and collected I'll read your opinions
and the passion will be gone   the passion will be gone
and I'll be ordered
and ready
to continue
in this numbing normality......
this nummmmm
          ummmm

23

I used to wonder why it took people so long to reply
Until I became that guy and considered all my reasons
And when I'm not sleeping or making an attempt at pro-
gressing
I'm second guessing the content of my message
and wishing we could meet in person
How long as it been since I was last seen?
On the scene since 18 and never really sure
If I preferred the way things were before
The grass is always greener
and the grains are perfect gold
on the other threshing floor
what's behind door number 4
on the game show that is
your fucking life
your only one
that at times it feels you're locked outside of and still
trying to get into
Let me know when you've found my groove
and I'll dance all night to rhythm of the moon
as the water in my body helps me wash away the blues
and wave goodbye to all that's bad to me
in search of something new

I want to find your grooves,
watch minds move
and ideas entwine.
I want to see each raindrop of your pain,
I want to hear the ring of your longing
and warm my hands
next to the fire of your love.

I don't want to misunderstand you.
I don't want to misunderstand you.

But I worry that I will.
Everything is red and raw
and in me, there's no still
I am lying on the floor,
shaking and exposed,
my left eye twitches,
and I notice it's open,
not closed.

I NEEDLE YOU

From: Lily Ashley
Sent: 29 November 2016 08:08
To: Grace Pilkington
Cc: James Massiah
Subject: Re: Hell-p me

junk fills my brain
but won't go insane
cos its a clear sky and a clear my oh my, bye bye
love, i've gone off it,
respecting situations wishing for validation
but it's coming
cos i respect you

and me
i respect you and me
and the clear blue means

 i can see

up before the rest
not a sex pest
not a sex pest
wanna fuck me best
best interest
best interest
gone off the rest.
wanna fuck me best

YES YES YES,
to best interest.
And fucking the best,
put all else to rest.
My mind is snugged in a vest,
and I feel excited about all to come,
dancing to the beat of my own heart drum,
a sound which was out of rhythm,
pallid for a while
but it's hard not to smile,
with blue skies,
and air crisper than Walkers.

And PS. G, coming to get ya.

firstly
it might be worth saying
that so many are full of shit
secondly
i realised that at certain times
i too have been full of it
but from my first breath to my last
asleep at peace in bed
or at war in a blood bath
i will be the best version of me
that i ever could have been
at times it's best to lie
break rules and bullshit
betraying rules of thumb
handed down by our forebears
but what a burden
i'm funky, free and fucked up
wading through the shit
off a bean and finally coming clean
bearing my soul as we lay
on these sex stained sheets

On our sex stained sheets?
Ours?
Or yours?
Dad wants you to be his son in law
Will say no more
My bed's raw
Of passion,
Love on ration,
It's out of fashion,
For me, for me.
You see, I think I'm free of panic
Panic of sexless bed
Panic of loveless head
Panic of going out on the push
(Opposing on the pull) and it feels so lush
Lush to see people just as them
Not as women not as men
Not as mine
Not as his
Not as hers
NOT TO KISS
Just to speak
Enjoy
And laugh
To work and make and break and craft
And no longer wear seduction mask
Just friendships built to last and last

GOING OUT
ON THE
PUSH

29

From: Grace Pilkington
Sent: 05 December 2016 14:05
To: James Massiah; Lily Ashley
Subject: Fw: Hell-p me

You seduce me with your words,
So empowered,
I cowered in a sex stained sheet,
Like I was dressing as a ghost on Halloween,
Trick or treat, Trick or treat,
Give me a man for my sheet,
I'd envelope them, suck them in,
And then the scarper game would begin,
Who can get free first?
Who can escape?
Pretence of love quickly becoming hate.
I decanted my seduction mask into a hip flask,
Not just for an emergency, but permanent company.
There was an urgency to the way I used to fill my bed.
But it's fuller than before, and lying in it is only one,
I watch his eyes close and his face rise with the sun.

No son yet for me
and no daughter, though it seems
that old school friends and church friends
have now their progeny
saw smiley in the ends
shotting ami got some bits
i told him i don't smoke
though i'm quite into partying
he laughed and said that times have changed
the brother's moving on!
and his daughters turning three
is going to pick her up from mums
what a life and what a world!
and what a time this life has been
my children still in neverland
the future's still a dream

A dream
A nightmare
A reality
My family
Flames
Her destiny
To burn
And yearn
And turn to coal
Up in flames to release her soul
My auntie maddened into death
Search the site there is nothing left
Her body and house and all with in
My mother her closest next of kin
My auntie died
In fire
Last night
And didn't notice
From drink so tight

From: James Massiah
Sent: 07 December 2016 17:17
To: Lily Ashley
Cc: Grace Pilkington
Subject: Re: Hell-p me

that's hard to hear
and cold to read
sending love
as loved ones grieve

On 7 Dec 2016, at 17:27, Grace Pilkington wrote:

Oh Lily, I'm sorry,
I hope you're okay,
sending endless love your way

xxx

From: Lily Ashley
Sent: 09 December 2016 15:15
To: Grace Pilkington
Cc: James Massiah
Subject: Re: Hell-p me

..........I'm sorry for writing the most emails
I'm sorry for dropping such sharp lines
I'm sorry for being so unbearably open
I'm sorry for saying sorry and sorry
I'm sorry if I stole your line, Grace
Didn't you say that?
Or was it Kane?

I'm cheerful today

By the way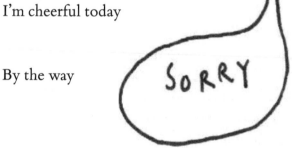

From: Grace Pilkington
Sent: 09 December 2016 17:52
To: Lily Ashley
Cc: James Massiah
Subject: Re: Hell-p me

hahahaha,
I wish.
Please steal my lines,
Kanye's vibe is a little unhinged, but fuck it, so is mine,
I want a bell to chime every time
I make a rhyme,
instead I've just got a headache
from yesterday's wines,
some guy was launching his book,
so I decided to indulge,
now my stomach is starting to bulge,
with all the cheddar I've consumed,
my healthy cottage life is doomed.
There was a Shoot out near Shoot up Hill,
bodies filling with bullets
and all I can say is, I'm full

READ
THAT WRONG
DIDNT YA!
KANE NOT KANYE

From: James Massiah
Sent: 12 December 2016 13:59
To: Grace Pilkington; Lily Ashley
Subject: Re: Hell-p me

and thank fuck for good fortune
i could always do with more
but for now i feel i'm fine
the cup is half way full
and i'm not suffering for fools
=gold is the goal and i'm strolling up the field
to the halfway house
the halfway line
will take us through
from 12 till 2
and beyond
till the moon
disappears
and our fears
climb back to the surface
but suppress those woes
with a cup of water
a pre-sleep paracetamol
and a loved one to spoon
in the absence of the night nurse
i say good morning to all you
merry motherfuckers!
stretch out, wank off and yawn
this is a brand new dawn

It dawned on me,
recently,
that I'd chased too many dawns,
the red glowing light,
rising through houses,
peering over trees,
I'd gobbled it up,
drunk it down,
while it charred and crisped my stomach.
My mum was a dawn chaser,
and was scalded by its fire,
I've tried to rise with it instead,
inhale and
exhale and
try to keep my empty cup full.
But as it's Christmas time,
I'll fill it with mulled wine,
and through frosty and grey skies,
I'll try to find a dawn,
chat to it till it yawns.
I'll peel tangerines like it's obscene
and get twerky with a turkey,
and then order some gear,
chat childhood with a reindeer,
and when I'm not harking the herald,
a ding donging or away in a manger,
I'll be in Sussex keeping out of danger.

Staying with strangers
And strangers staying with you
Eating stuffing till you're blue
But this year it'll be vegan
Roasted potatoes and tofu
For you
And you will not receive a gift
But a kiss
And no tree for me
Just a solar powered string of lights
A home knitted pair of tights
And some stroppy sister fights
To warm the stormy nights
Bless this and bless that
Felted mat
Overfed cat
Going to midnight mass this year
Dear mum needs support from the Lord
Bored of not believing
Heaving us to church
Helping us to purge
Purge our sins
Light within
So next year we will.....win

i'm doing alright
without some of the 'lights' a party in the dark of a
clapton warehouse
helped transform a crush into a cuddle on the sofa
in the company of the beloved
busta rhymes projected on a wall
fried chicken on our fingers
rum and ginger beer on our tongues
talking taste in music and musing on the future
of the movement
new ideas with these humans
helping me to push through
and so we labour
waiting for pay
as we pass through into the next chamber

It's in the air
Let's not call it love
But understanding
Hold handing
He curled over his stomach in the mist
Aimed his piss but missed
By the river
We discussed in a heated car
Bonnet making love to the junction
Straddling the white lines
Like minds
And now the chamomile
The flowers in their cups
Are pushed to the side
Reminding me
Quite happily
Of last night's ride.

From: Grace Pilkington

Sent: 20 December 2016 23:55

To: Lily Ashley

Cc: James Massiah

Subject: Re: Hell-p me

Who's this guy?
Who's this guy?
Chamomile flowers and calm, I've been
Rubbing lavender balm on wrists,
And singing psalms,
Avoiding people,
Apart from one.
Discussing ideas and fears
And what the coming years
Will hold.
What if I get
Restless
And old
Fidgeting
Shaking
For the body of another,
For their sweat, their voice,
Their weight on top of me,
Their silhouette on the wall,
What if I want another?
What if I can't do monogamy
And discuss wallpaper and mahogany?
Does it scare you?
It scares me.
But I know who I want to try it with,
And I will keep trying
And will make sure I succeed,
Because all else is tumble weed.

tumbling tumbling tumbling
time is
tumbling down a mountain
sisyphus is tumbling
pussyfoot
tumbling
tumbling
tumbling
tumbling
time to...

Fumble
Fumble
Fumble my words
My yearns
Your turn
Your turn
Here is the dice now fucking roll
No I'm the troll
You're the

Forget it
Let's not play
Not today
Wine yes
Nice dress
Fixed my shoes
Now can use
Destabilised in heels
Your turn to deal...

From: Grace Pilkington
Sent: 24 December 2016 21:30
To: Lily Ashley
Cc: James Massiah
Subject: Re: Hell-p me

It was my turn to deal,
When I span on my heel,
Unrolling a wheel
Of yarn,
I never meant any harm,
But he found it in my actions,
Scanned my doings with his eyes.
Now it's different,
When photocopier eyes
Flash
They find only love.
Today we sat around reading books,
8 girls, 1 boy,
Now 8 women and one man,
We moved towards the table,
Munched potatoes and ham,
Uncomfortable in the world usually,
But here at ease.
At ease.
As 2016 starts to cease

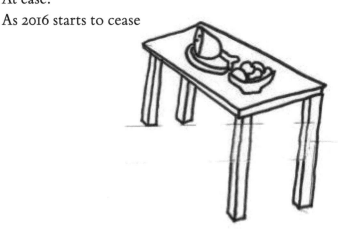

I ate so much
And drunk so much
I saw daylight
But not that much

I danced so much
And sang so much
And slept at night
But not that much

We talked so much
And walked so much
We thought we might
But not that much

Got high so much
And 'died' so much
Did what was right
For us, so much

So much consumed,
I wrestled through rooms,
looking for shiny chocolates,
in glittery wrappers,
and flicked through channels
in a frantic manner,
my shirt burst open,
and my jeans popped,
but I couldn't be stopped,
Like a wild boar,
I sniffed out more,
to guzzle,
hoard in my stomach,
all in preparation for hibernation,
all routes go via glutton Station,
Santa's sacks hang underneath my eyes,
and my arteries bubble with wine,
Greasy skin pricked with pine,
It's no wonder I feel far from fine.

I've got into Angel cards and they all read greed
Suppress and address this weird sugar need
I am lying on my back with a tummy full of shake
I wanna go to sleep but it's keeping me awake
And I can't concentrate on the important things to do
Cos I'm stuck down on the bed with super glue
And the super glue is a mix of all that food I just gobbled
And the long walk home I forced myself to hobble
The combination of over eating then over exercising
Drawing out the days between being born and dying
Drawing out the days, tempting us to tire
So we don't call them out for being a liar
But who the fuck is them? It's only fucking me
Letting myself down, focused on a he
Again a he but HE's the one
Fuck
Ah I'm a fucking stuck track
8 fucking years
I keep going back
It's him it's him it's him
It's always fucking him
That makes me shorten skirts and give my armpit hair a trim
That has never grossed me out unlike all the other twats
Who've talked big of love and life who've I've had on their backs
He oh he's the only one who I can't exist without
Who I'd sacrifice a fuck just to have about
Who seems so dope and cool but couldn't be shyer
Who when he swings me round he always swings me higher

48

From: Lily Ashley
Sent: 13 January 2017 20:08
To: Grace Pilkington
Cc: James Massiah
Subject: Re: Hell-p me

Email back!
Email back!
I'm going insane
Email back!
Email back!
The nights take my brain
My dreams!
My dreams!
Make me feel I'm regressing
Visions of the past
Feelings I'm repressing

On 13 Jan 2017, at 22:26, Grace Pilkington
wrote:

I watch the words you write,
see them in their paper flight,
soaring, whilst the world,
applauding,
and staring as
feathers of purple and gold
spin through the sky.
I'll try,
I'l try,

Progression over regression,
I say, still lamenting old obsessions,
I let apparitions hover at my bed,
and past frustrations fill my head,
I never move forward only backwards,
or slightly to the side,
with Fumble and Fall
rather than Glide.
Move forward,
I resolutely decided on the eve of the new year,
Get my book out of its cobwebbed cyber folder,
Be Better,
Be Better,
Be Better,
and
Be Bolder.

From: James Massiah
Sent: 16 January 2017 10:42
To: Grace Pilkington (forgot Lily by accident)
Subject: Re: Hell-p me

You should see my cyber girlfriend
And all the freaky things we do
In the meantime, my actual girlfriend
In the surreal world, doesn't see me much at all!

Words on a screen,
Words on a screen,
Words on a screen,

A world in a screen,
A world in a screen,
A world in a screen,
She sets me free.

Be bolder and follow through
The year is new
The near is you
And I just watched Eileen Myles
(She said she changed names for privacy
But I will keep hers)
Cos I am desperate to be...
To be
COOL
At least that is what I screamed
At the gaze
Of a woman who bowled me over
A woman whose voice glowed low and slow
And what do you know
I'm gay again
Game again
For her, or him
Or was it them
Ten of ten
For them
She caught me on her earring
Now I'm stuck in her hair
Not Myles but not miles away
Another pine to wine a day

(A CLiMBiNM
CLiP... i MEAN,
PLEASE, So COOL)

Boulders and miles,
And tall, dancing pines,
Shaking their heads
At my terrible rhymes.
I want to be cool,
To be cool and laid back,
But I'm lying back,
My back is against the sheet
But the Insomniac is prowling,
It has tried counting sheep,
Or so they seem to be,
But they're rougher,
Tougher,
They're stray dogs howling
And growling I wait
Patiently for sleep,
It's the jailor and
I'm in its keep,
It taunts me and won't let me free,
I hear its footsteps
And the clink of its keys,
Lids feel heavy,
Lids feel heavy,
Heavy, Heaving even,
Heavenly, Heavenly sleep,
Come here, Come here,
I know you're near.

I'm Still Awake.

Awake again
And gay again
In previous poems
My pen has played
With the meaning
Of them
Friend in the streets
Asks me if I'm fine
I'm fine as a Ferrari
On a double red line
But when will I get mine?
I sleep Again
And Dream
Again
Are you happy
My friend?

From: Lily Ashley

Sent: 25 January 2017 17:04

To: Grace Pilkington

Cc: James Massiah

Subject: Re: Hell-p me

I'm happy
As happy as my beating heart
And the fingers penetrating my ears
And the panting breath
Yes
I'm happy
Haaaaaaaa-pppppeeee
Aassssss-eeeee
Laaaaaa-reeee
I'm angry
I'm angry
The world is angry
Can't sleep so I dance through my night
Not at a nightclub
In my room
To a ballet tutorial's repetitive tune
But it tires me out and means I can sleep
so knackered that my dreams don't make a peak
cos I was trapped in a rhythm of vivid nightmares
highlighting quite how much I care
about the empty space next door in bed
the plumped up pillow, no foreign head
to squish it and squish me
the weight of an arm with a hand
to hold in my sweaty palm.

From: Grace Pilkington

Sent: 25 January 2017 17:29

To: Lily Ashley

Cc: James Massiah

Subject: Re: Hell-p me

Sweaty Palms
Pursed Lips
Sweaty Palms
Pursed Lips
Sweaty Palms
Pursed Palms
Sweaty Lips.

I am trying
Not to engage
With the rage
And focus on
My page

From: James Massiah
Sent: 26 January 2017 12:28
To: Grace Pilkington; Lily Ashley
Subject: Re: Hell-p me

Sweaty palms
Thinking about my purse
About to make another purchase
What kind of person do I want to be
And how do I wanna be perceived
As I prance around in this world
My creps need to be comfortable
Enough for me to dance and expensive
Enough to say, I've advanced in my career
And I've arrived goddamit!
I'm a man! Who works hard!
And fights hard for what he's earned!
Despite knowledge of the fact there's
Plenty of evidence to the contrary
In the shape of our quiet strolling down
New Oxford street discussing pegging
You have foul intentions for me
Belinda's are clean
In pony hair shoes
Brand new

Adrenaline pumped
Through my tyred body,
Sugar curdled in my throat.
Like a petal on a fluffy cocktail,
I'd like to drift and float,
But.
I'm not that light,
But I do like,
Attention,
Avenues of faces
Voices speaking
Different tones,
Different paces,
And watching.
The next day I feel deflated,
I think,
'God – writing is overrated'
It's like an ache that roams through
My body,
I can't not do it.
I could never not do it.
My fingers itch
To eclipse white paper with ink,
But in all this ink and all these words,
There are only a few moments when it doesn't hurt,
When I'm addled with adrenaline and fixed on my face
        is a sick grin,
Only a few moments when it feels completely right,
And one of them was performing with you two last night.

From: Lily Ashley
Sent: 07 February 2017 19:38
Subject: Re: Hell-p me

wasn't it great!   wasn't it...
               ..i'm fine   ...i'm fine
    ...i lied   the come down came quicker
hit across the pitter patter screen
leaned
around and over the steering wheel
curled around where i could feel
the loneliness
and suck it up and out
my tears became a shout
the world tilted ajar
hobbled past my shuddering car
and looked back and in
what pray within

paranoid and alone
i look to empty home   strangers walk towards the door
i knew it, they've come back for more
they weren't happy with what they stole
they're coming back to catch my soul

my sweaty palm vibrates my phone
why am i always alone?   alone alone in see through dress
with darting eyes, a batty mess
and through my fear leaps out a sound
so unhinged they turn around

oh what to do i'm in no state...   ...i realise it's my house mate
and her boyfriend, there was a change of plan
they're staying this side of town
my shoulders drop my arms fly wide
i spring to them with bouncing stride
and in the kitchen they give advice
on i can't remember but it was nice
and i'm so happy to be with friends
i forget
i forget
i forget it ends

And end it did
another night alone
My love
If only it weren't so
Things must be the way they be
And if they change that's how they be
Edie saw me necking
in peckham my lady friend wants more but i'm not qualified to give
Afraid that she will live alone
frustrated i won't lay
but we all know what they say
too many lights in the bush
spoil the broth of birds
when a stitch in time could
save nine lives because
it's bad luck when the mirror
breaks seven times
under a ladder on the day
of the dead if it's the 13th
when love is the root of all evil
money is the answer to
be or not to bother me
because it's tough at the bottom
of the topsy turvy world
that makes it go round

Or some words to that effect
Whatever it was
I can't wait to see you next

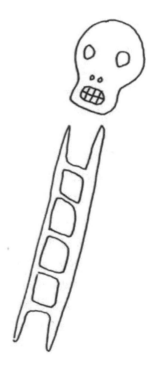

61

From: Lily Ashley
Sent: 08 February 2017 15:42
To: James Massiah
Cc: Grace Pilkington
Subject: Re: Hell-p me

To be or not to bother me
James wow wee

Confessed again
Now ashamed I loved
Unrequited as expected
Whatever, heart still protected
Still positioned
Still in chest
Freed from loving one the best
Back to poly
Back to lots
To selfish
To selfless
To all forgot
To you are me
And I am you
To doing what I want to do
No longer stuck with super glue
To caring what and where and who
And now I will be free like you
Like you James, free, free like you

From: Grace Pilkington
Sent: 08 February 2017 16:21
To: Lily Ashley; James Massiah
Subject: Re: Hell-p me

To be free,

to tear self off where super glued,
before own life becomes skewed,
and is only for another.
Yes to being or not being bothered.
If like me you've hovered in naked flames,
you're going to get scorched every once in a while.
The flame, the heat pricking the skin, does beguile,
But then when asked to wait in single file,
I laugh with a crooked smile
WAIT? I can't wait.
It's NOW or never,
which often means never,
and I do endeavour
to take things slowly,
to have more confidence
in my competence.

But right now, I am standing in a fortress,
wearing an iron armour dress,
I fear my mind is on the attack,
against my body,
which feels overworked and underplayed,
And has known to lie splayed
when the mind's troops start to invade.

From: James Massiah
Sent: 13 February 2017 09:34
To: Grace Pilkington; Lily Ashley
Subject: Re: Hell-p me

Play away for days and days
Do it if it feels okay
The battle is between
Both your body and your brain
If only to unite the twain
And make Descartes turn in his grave
Sometime soon we'll find a way
For soul and flesh to separate

Descartes, Days Carted away,
Another gone, carted, departed,
I didn't even realise it had started?
The day of St Valentine
Sends shivers of cringe up my spine.
But then I feel like a cynical git,
For passionately hating on it.
But it seems designed to make you feel shit.
'Excuse me, if you please, I'm armed with cheese
And coming on through

And my smirking teddy bear and squeaky balloon
Are bigger than you.'
I have to say, dualism fails me today,
As my stomach twists with pain,
And my gums ache,
And each night I wake,
With the weight of my mind,
Heavy on this body of mine.

Yesterday, what a prick
What national abuse!
The only day of the year
I chug chocolate mousse

It's not that I care
I've been hypnotised
That is why I'm affected
All my childhood, on this day
Counting love notes I'd collected

From mum
And dad
And evil friends
Making out I had secret admirers
With roses and sweets and handwritten cards so I
Never expected a liar.

I've broken up three times
With three separate loves
On v day d day of the heart
Maybe that is why I glug?

I love you more than ever
Specifically today
And to help you understand
I'm gonna pay and pay and pay

For out of season roses
And out of season berries
And champagne unsold from Christmas
So we can fake that we are merry

And all the ones rejecting
Say 'it's just a normal day
Society is making money
And it's us who must obey

Well it's not a normal day
Even if you have rejected
Cos you never call days 'normal'
So you must have been affected

Normally these things don't affect me
But when I'd heard about her
Hanging out with homeboy
On the low
It caught me kinda different
Not quite a belly blow
More like a little spike
That had pricked me on the wrist
Reminded me I never give much thought to it
Monogamy and other such
Trinkets for the heart
This little thing had ended
And it didn't even start

From: Lily Ashley
Sent: 19 February 2017 19:01
To: James Massiah
Cc: Grace Pilkington
Subject: Re: Hell-p me

But who defines a start
And who defines an end?
Right now your mood feels wonky
But you haven't lost a friend
And I guarantee she digs you
But girls are way more smart
And she'd of seen your ability
To break her willing heart
Cos even though you feel a loss
If she was waiting on a platter
Maybe you'd of never felt it
So I think it doesn't matter
You have the joy of a companion
Who can mature into a lover
Who'll entertain you with her mind
Although she's tied up with another

On 21 Feb 2017, at 17:34, Grace Pilkington
wrote:

She defined my start,
and she'll define the end,
I am nauseous and out of sleep,
And last night I lay to weep,
Because between mother and daughter
Is a bond too deep,
But is it only me who knows?
Her blood bubbles and flows,
With addiction and depression,
Each word a painful confession,
And I try to be sympathetic,
cock my head and say 'poor you',
but she turns my insides askew,
with rage, frustration and love,
because she decided long ago,
that she'd had enough,
but after shedding skins, I saw
that she is at my core,
and whatever she is able to give,
I will always want more.

From: Lily Ashley
Sent: 23 February 2017 15:50
To: Grace Pilkington
Cc: James Massiah
Subject: Re: Hell-p me

More more
The desperate claw
Attached to her, can't not adore
Mother mother mother mother
Calls me up, 'hello Mumma
What's that noise in the back ground
It's making a really jarring sound
...you're washing up? Ah I see
But why are you calling me?
Yes I saw, yes I've liked it
50 likes? Wow that's quick!
Mum that sound is really sharp
Smacking my head like a dart
...no sorry, it's just you know, the moon is waning
I'm feeling quite a lot of pain and..
...yes, exactly, that time of the month
That noise! I wanna fucking punch..!
Yea, thanks mum, you understand,
B-bye, I love you' the phone is slammed
And I'm wound up like a toy train
But the anger was refrained
And I pat myself on my back
For not becoming my usual prat
And blaming all my pain on ma
Cos she always pushes a little too far.

71

From: James Massiah
Sent: 28 February 2017 09:14
To: Lily Ashley; Grace Pilkington
Subject: Re: Hell-p me

Zsa Zsa
Mother, wife and house keeper supreme
We've love in mind
And an affair with a stepchild
The proof was in the homemade pudding
Philip Larkin was true
They fuck you up they do!
I'm looking to mine for a leg up
Which is only fair considering how
Tricky they've made it for me to enjoy
Getting a leg over

I was slow like the hour hand
Rushing and rushing
In thought but not deed
Our love is now dying

Larkin, So stark in
observations
about frustrations,
He was right,
Old school hats sat
on old school heads,
and it's with their cutlery that I'm still fed,
A scratched up silver spoon,
flying into my mouth,
Like an aeroplane,
Perhaps I can use it to knock the pain on the head,
Like a hard boiled egg,
and dip crusty, toasted bread in and watch the yolk
ooze, a thick yellow cruise, bright and sickly
like disappointment at my imperfection,
and my longing for her affection,
it stains the bread and then the corners of my mouth
and every word now is slightly yellow-tinted, yellow-dyed,
and I'm sorry but I can't put bread analogies aside,
I'm told I am no longer allowed it as it makes me ill,
But now I fill every moment with dreams of a fleet of wheat,
ciabatta, pasta and pizza, and oh fuck I want a fajita.

SCRATCHED UP SILVER SPOON

From: Lily Ashley
Sent: 05 March 2017 11:01
To: Grace Pilkington
Cc: James Massiah
Subject: Re: Hell-p me

I'd like a fajita but the grubs been stashed
I'm up a lane in the rain and I've got no cash
I've gotta leave, gotta work, gotta get shit done
But I feel like this holiday only just begun
Yes they fuck you up
But we fuck them up too
Reflections of what they did and didn't do
A mirror to the addictions that they didn't cleanse
Imperfection and mistakes through a super zoom lens
It's not our fault – it is the dreams that we are sold
Buying up a myth that young is stupid, wise is old
Buying into torture cos we have no time to think
And we'd prefer to drown our sorrows in the poison of a drink.

From: Grace Pilkington

Sent: 14 March 2017 14:17

To: Lily Ashley

Cc: James Massiah

Subject: Re: Hell-p me

Yes – they are not better, purer, more on top of it
    and less confused,
They've only had longer on here; more time to get
    cut and bruised.
I've laid expectations like a chicken lays eggs, they pop
    out everywhere,
I don't even notice, they come out so quick – one here,
    two over there.
Like eggs, they're fragile, easily cracked and rarely hatch,
Sometimes I'll chuck them up high and scream 'CATCH!'
They'll go spinning through the air and land on the floor
    with a crack and a smash,
Where I'll be waiting, one hand on hip, the other with a
    whip ready for the backlash.
'How could this happen?' I'll say, staring glumly at the mess.
'Who is responsible, come on you – it's your fault, confess!'
Why did you have to let me down?
Why couldn't you just let me throw you around,
Imagine you were real and coming to fruition,
Why did you put ME in this awkward position?
But the truth is, it wouldn't have cracked had I not
    thrown it up high,
Had I not taken it everywhere and let it become
    the apple of my eye.
If I'd just laid an expectation and casually walked away,
Without clenching my fists with anticipation day after day,
Then there's a chance it might have actually been okay.

THE EGG
OF
EXPECTATION

If I could only say,
it's nothing to do with me,
it is after all a separate entity,
Then perhaps I'd be the kind of person I aimed to be,
    at the beginning of this verse,

Who talks about the bright sky and the warm duvet air –
    someone accurate and terse
But very sadly,
I went off on
some weird egg analogy.

Egg analogies
Remind me
Of the story
Of the eye

A mother walks in
A priest sins
An egg cracks
Inside a not-so virgin
When in flight
I need books to read
Give sex, give me violence
Give me guts, give me greed
All the pleasures of the flesh
All the evil, all the lust
The things our keepers
Desire to hide from us

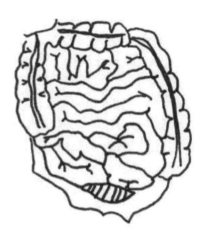

The Story of The Eye,
The eggs and when she dips
Herself in a saucer of white cream,
'Milk is for the pussy isn't it?'
She asks,
I was fifteen
When my older boyfriend handed me the book,
I read a few pages and was quickly hooked.
He wanted to lead the exploration of my sexuality,
Like an Estate Agent might show someone around a house,
But I was timid like a mouse,
And not ready to see the attic.
My insides ached with love for him,
I laid myself out
Like a sacrificed lamb,
And believed everything he told me I am
He taught me words,
To replace school's education,
With which I had become impatient
Once we even looked up Paedophile,
To find he in fact was one, oh how we smiled.
The story of I
And him
Began to fall apart,
And I was left with a leaking heart.

From: Lily Ashley
Sent: 18 March 2017 17:19
To: Grace Pilkington
Cc: James Massiah
Subject: Re: Hell-p me

A leaking heart is better than sealed
Made of steel and stolen back
Defend, defend, do not attack!
Pretend, pretend, you like them so
But 'I've given up, so sorry, no'
8 days late and now I'm spent
No longer love notes being sent
No longer pining, no 'hoo hoo'
(A little joke, Grace, that's for you!)
'Yahoo!' leaps lady in my chest
I love me best. I love me best.

From: James Massiah
Sent: 19 March 2017 12:30
To: Lily Ashley; Grace Pilkington
Subject: Re: Hell-p me

'All love is self-love...'
Says the text
A contraction
True, a fact
Too many
Not enoughs
What? Yes
Long time
No see
No. Seen?
Yes. Replied
In bad time
Can't wait for
Another good one

All love is self-love, and to me, it's quite a surprise,
All the times I've said 'yous', but it's really been 'Is'
Like the time a month ago when I was disappointed and hurt,
I decided to wipe my own mother callously through the dirt,
My implication was that she was to blame,
For all the reasons I get sick with anxiety and go insane,
And since that day I've squirmed with the thought
That if read, my words could make our relationship fraught,
I feel uncomfortable with the feelings and can barely sit,
With the idea that I could make my mother sound unfit,
A cruel thing when I was squashed into her womb,
Kicking my feet and punching my fists for room,
They found that I was the wrong way round.
She was sliced open and etched on her stomach is the permanent scar,
The reminder that she carried me into existence, that she brought
        me this far,
And I cannot demean her strength when she held me and holds
        me still,
Nor attack her for being human, for getting lost, for being ill.
But every day, I drift in and out of feelings like a piece of wood
        at sea,
Sure and solid that this is reality, the truth, this is definitely me,
And then the wind changes the direction and I'm in lighter, warmer
        waters with land in view,
The fury dissipates and fades away and so this is why I can talk about
        'I' and never 'you'

81

From: Lily Ashley
Sent: 23 March 2017 11:08
To: Grace Pilkington
Cc: James Massiah
Subject: Re: Hell-p me

This world breeds anxiety
It's not your fault
War on terror
But terror is taught
A drill on the tube
And I loose my face
My heart does press ups
With trembling pace
And though I feel, weakly, satisfied
When death came close I asked her why?
Why them?
      Why this?
Why now, this day?
Why me?
What if?
I'm not okay!
With this, right now, my work's undone...
And how? A knife? A car? A gun?
But now sat safe on thundering train
Late for work, I'll work, again
And is it life I am waiting for?
Or death?
Is it terror terrorising?
Or safety saving our souls and selling them to time?

I got the fucking train two days in a row
And remembered why I ride
Hate being trapped inside
Some shit head's taken sick
Well now I'm gonna be late you prick
Vomit on the
Victoria Line
Everyone on this train better be just fine
Cos I ain't got time
I just can't wait
Think twice between
Putting a dodgy dish on your plate
When it's half past eight
And you're home from work
Microwave that shit and get rid of the germs
Cos it's rush hour now
And last night's bug
Is here on the underground to fuck my shit up
But hey
At least I'm alive I suppose
With work to go to
And my runny nose
(At least it still works)
sniff sniff *snuff snuff*
Ooh! Look at that red lever
I wonder what that does?

With thanks to: Todd Swift, Rosanna Hildyard and the Eyewear team for their efficiency and belief in our vision. To Chingis Guirey for creating this extraordinary cover image. To Genevieve Garner and Storm Collective for their endless support. To Lily Bertrand-Webb for being so brilliant behind a camera and snapping us in the bath. To all the Ashleys for their unwavering enthusiasm and for letting us rehearse and perform in their sitting room. To all the Pilkingtons for always being there and loving it. To Conrad Gamble for hosting us at Ear Smoke and to all our friends for supporting us and laughing at all the right moments. And with special thanks from Grace to Fred Armesto for his unfaltering love and support and his recent promise of a lifetime of it.

Little Grape Jelly is the poetry collective of Lily
Ashley, Grace Pilkington and James Massiah.
Lily first sent the words 'Hell-p Me' in an email to
Grace and James in July 2016, establishing an online
space where anything could be shared, through the
medium of poetry. This is their correspondence:
unedited, uncensored and spontaneous, via email
and social media over the past ten months. In free
verse and other poetry forms, the work details
the ups and downs of life and love in the digital
age, and explores the benefits and limitations of
communicating online. Immediate, honest and
fleeting, here is what happens when three different
worlds collide on one page.

Editors' note: This book has been thoroughly proofread,
and edited, by Rosanna Hildyard, Alexandra Payne, and
Todd Swift. The editorial aim was to very much respect the
poetic plan to represent the original 'heat of the moment'
compositional nature of the process. Each page has been
considered as its own aesthetic event, and no overall house
style or consistency has been overlaid on the whole – thus
any non-errors that have crept in are entirely the fault of
the editors.

UU **EYEWEAR** PUBLISHING

EYEWEAR
POETRY

ELSPETH SMITH DANGEROUS CAKES
CALEB KLACES BOTTLED AIR
GEORGE ELLIOTT CLARKE ILLICIT SONNETS
HANS VAN DE WAARSENBURG THE PAST IS NEVER DEAD
BARBARA MARSH TO THE BONEYARD
DON SHARE UNION
SHEILA HILLIER HOTEL MOONMILK
MARION MCCREADY TREE LANGUAGE
SJ FOWLER THE ROTTWEILER'S GUIDE TO THE DOG OWNER
AGNIESZKA STUDZINSKA WHAT THINGS ARE
JEMMA BORG THE ILLUMINATED WORLD
KEIRAN GODDARD FOR THE CHORUS
COLETTE SENSIER SKINLESS
ANDREW SHIELDS THOMAS HARDY LISTENS TO LOUIS ARMSTRONG
JAN OWEN THE OFFHAND ANGEL
A.K. BLAKEMORE HUMBERT SUMMER
SEAN SINGER HONEY & SMOKE
HESTER KNIBBE HUNGERPOTS
MEL PRYOR SMALL NUCLEAR FAMILY
ELSPETH SMITH KEEPING BUSY
TONY CHAN FOUR POINTS FOURTEEN LINES
MARIA APICHELLA PSALMODY
TERESE SVOBODA PROFESSOR HARRIMAN'S STEAM AIR-SHIP
ALICE ANDERSON THE WATERMARK
BEN PARKER THE AMAZING LOST MAN
MANDY KAHN MATH, HEAVEN, TIME
ISABEL ROGERS DON'T ASK
REBECCA GAYLE HOWELL AMERICAN PURGATORY
MARION MCCREADY MADAME ECOSSE
MARIELA GRIFFOR DECLASSIFIED
MARK YAKICH THE DANGEROUS BOOK OF POETRY FOR PLANES
HASSAN MELEHY A MODEST APOCALYPSE
KATE NOAKES PARIS, STAGE LEFT
JASON LEE BURNING BOX
U.S. DHUGA THE SIGHT OF A GOOSE GOING BAREFOOT
DICK WITTS THE PASSAGE: POST-PUNK POETS